The Common Core Readiness Guide to Reading™

TIPS & TRICKS FOR DETERMINING POINT OF VIEW AND PURPOSE

Sandra K. Athans and Robin W. Parente

ROSEN PUBLISHING®
New York

Published in 2015 by The Rosen Publishing Group, Inc.
29 East 21st Street, New York, NY 10010

First Edition

Library of Congress Cataloging-in-Publication Data

Athans, Sandra K., 1958–
Tips & tricks for determining point of view and purpose/Sandra K. Athans and Robin W. Parente. — First Edition.
pages cm.—(The Common Core Readiness Guide to Reading)
Includes bibliographical references and index.
Audience: Grades 5-8.
ISBN 978-1-4777-7555-4 (library bound) — ISBN 978-1-4777-7557-8 (pbk.) — ISBN 978-1-4777-7558-5 (6-pack)
1. Perspective (Linguistics)—Juvenile literature. 2. Point of view (Literature)—Juvenile literature. 3. Critical thinking—Juvenile literature. 4. Creative thinking—Juvenile literature. 5. Readers (Middle school) I. Parente, Robin W. II. Title. III. Title: Tips and tricks for determining point of view and purpose.
P302.76.A75 2015
372.47'2—dc23

2014007399

Manufactured in the United States of America

Contents

Introduction

The Common Core Reading Standards are a set of skills designed to prepare you for entering college or beginning your career. They're grouped into broad College and Career Readiness Anchor Standards, and they help you use reasoning and evidence in ways that will serve you well now and in the future.

The skills build from kindergarten to the twelfth grade. Grades 6 through 8 take the spotlight here. You may already have noticed changes in your classrooms that are based on the standards—deeper-level reading, shorter passages, an emphasis on informational texts, or an overall increase in rigor within your daily activities.

This book will help you understand, practice, and independently apply the skills through easy-to-use "tips and tricks." Gaining mastery of the skills is the goal.

Your teachers may use close reading for some of their instruction. During close reading, you read shorter passages more deeply and analytically.

Close-reading passages often have rich, complex content. They contain grade-level vocabulary words, sentence

The standards encourage students to read widely and deeply from a range of high-quality, increasingly challenging literature and informational texts.

structures, and literary techniques. Reading a short three-page passage closely could take two to three days or more. The benefit to you is that you get a deeper, more valuable understanding of what you've read. Close reading is a critical part of the new Common Core Reading Standards and is used throughout this book.

Other well-known reading comprehension skills remain valuable. Visualizing, asking questions, synthesizing, and other traditional strategies work well together with the Common Core skills covered here.

This book focuses on Anchor Standard 6: Assess "how point of view or purpose shapes the content and style of a text." In the next chapter, we'll break this standard apart and look at it closely. Also, the tips and tricks that can help you gain mastery of this standard are introduced.

In the passages that follow, you tag along with "expert readers" as they think aloud while closely reading different passages of literature (fiction) and informational text (nonfiction). Visual icons that represent the tips and tricks appear in the margins and prompt the expert reader. Ways in which the expert reader applies them appear in expert reader margin notes. You'll also observe the expert readers respond to multiple-choice questions and prepare written responses that demonstrate their assessment of point of view and how it shapes the content and style of a text.

After you gain an understanding of how the skills are applied, it's your turn to try with guided practice. You'll apply the skills independently and perform a self-evaluation by checking your responses against answers provided. Based on your responses, you can determine if another pass through the expert reader's examples might be helpful—or if you've mastered the skill.

CHAPTER 1

A QUICK AND EASY OVERVIEW: THE SKILLS AND THE TIPS & TRICKS

Let's examine the skills involved with determining point of view and purpose so that we understand it. We know the word "assess" is a verb, something we actively do. "Assess" means "to evaluate, determine, judge, or appraise." Point of view refers to the angle from which a story is told. It could also be the perspective an author takes on a topic based on his or her purpose or objectives. To assess the point of view and purpose of a text is therefore an analytical skill in which you identify the point of view and investigate how it develops and shapes the content or style of the text. Examining point of view enables you to look closely at the craft and structure of a text. This, in turn, helps build your comprehension.

As you examine point of view within a text, you may need to make inferences about ideas or events not explicitly stated. An inference is a conclusion you make by interpreting clues provided in the passage; it's as if you're reading between the lines. Your inferences must be reasonably based on something concrete in the text.

For works of literature, you will be assessing ways in which an author develops the point of view of the narrator or speaker in a text,

Your analysis of informational text may require that you examine and distinguish how conflicting views are presented and justified.

contrasts the views of multiple narrators or characters, or creates special effects through the use of point of view. For informational works, you'll determine the author's point of view, investigate how it's conveyed, and distinguish how conflicting views may be justified. As you shall see, there are mild nuances in the manner in which you apply this skill to the different genres. Yet, with practice, these adjustments become automatic.

As you progress in grade levels, you're expected to assess how authors develop point of view broadly. They may intend to contrast multiple characters' views, to stir readers' suspense or humor, or even to distinguish or address conflicting positions.

Tips & Tricks on Point of View

There are several easy-to-use tips and tricks that can help you identify and then analyze the treatment of point of view within a text. Some are useful as you begin to read, while others guide you throughout your reading. Here's a quick overview of them. The icons featured below are used in subsequent sections to show you how the tips and tricks are used in action with literature and informational texts.

- **Launching "Jump-Start" Clues:** Before you dive into reading a piece of text, skim it. Notice and take a visual inventory of everything you see. The title, subheadings, boldface print, and other features, like photographs or charts, will give you valuable clues about the content and genre. Authors select and use text features purposefully. It's often helpful to ask yourself, "What could the title mean or what purpose do the special features serve?" As you prepare to assess point of view, jump-starting your investigation by detecting the content and genre of each passage marks a good beginning.

- **Using Craft and Text Structure:** Looking closely at how authors of literature and informational text carefully construct, craft, and develop their ideas can help us gain a comprehensive understanding of a work and its unique style. Specifically determining how components such as sentences and paragraphs or lines and stanzas help develop theme, plot, or setting is a way for us to do this. Looking critically at smaller units of composition and explaining how they fit into the larger passage is like analyzing the many building materials used to construct a home—cement foundation, wooden framework, and sheetrock walls. Each contributes to the complete home. Uncovering how smaller ideas are developed into the larger passage helps us uncover how we construct meaning from a passage.

- **Identifying and Monitoring Point of View or Perspective and Being Attentive to the Author:** In literature, thinking about who is telling the story from the start, how the person is telling it, and what information he or she chose to impart helps you identify and monitor point of view. A story often unfolds through the eyes of a character (first person) or perhaps an unnamed narrator (third person). Authors determine this very carefully. As attentive readers, we must examine the storyteller through his or her actions and words (dialogue) and even how other characters may react to the storyteller in order to fully understand the text. Meanwhile, nonfiction and informational text is filtered through the author's perspective. Knowing this is important as you analyze what the author is saying and how he or she is presenting information. Also, determining the credibility of the author as a knowledgeable source and being attentive to the author while reading literature and informational text is critical.

- **Breaking Apart Literary Elements:** In works of literature, the characters, events, and setting of a story are among the literary elements that an author carefully crafts together to move the plot forward. Breaking apart and analyzing the literary elements separately aids our comprehension of the text and can also help us assess point of view. Determining how we witness events within the text is filtered through a character's or speaker's point of view.

  Elements found within informational text can also be broken apart for analysis. Here, authors may use examples, anecdotes, comparisons, analogies, or other methods to establish relationships between individuals, events, and ideas. Considering how an author has launched and developed information is key. Also keep in mind that authors of informational text have a point to make about a topic. They frequently want to shape our thinking and will use expository, procedural, or persuasive formats.

- **Tune In to Your Inside Voice:** Your mind is actively making sense as you read. Listening to your thoughts or your mind's dialogue helps you grasp meaning. Connecting new ideas to known ideas is the way your mind builds cohesive meaning. Monitoring your thoughts, including your questions, is critical. Is the narrator reliable? Do characters' motives, events in the story, or ideas seem unusual or out of place? Is the author swaying me with his or her argument? How do charts, tables, or other special features included within a passage build my understanding? Are my reactions likely what the author intended? Authors often build reader engagement by posing questions. However, it's also important for you to determine when you're confused and need to implement fix-up strategies like rereading.

- **Avoid Common Pitfalls:** Sometimes we can become distracted by something in the text, which could steer us away from an author's intended meaning. Staying engaged and focused while ensuring that your ideas square with text-based evidence is critical. It's sometimes helpful to validate your interpretation by considering how you would complete the following sentence: "I know this because . . ." Your answer to this question must be found within the passage. In analyzing point of view, it may be critical to distinguish and suspend your point of view from characters, narrators, or authors so that your analysis is not biased.

CHAPTER 2

DETERMINING POINT OF VIEW AND PURPOSE IN LITERATURE: EXPERT READER MODEL

Let's see how to apply the tips and tricks to literature. Remember literature can be adventure stories, historical fiction, mysteries, myths, science fiction, realistic fiction, and more.

Literature often features elements such as characters, problems or conflicts, a setting, events, and a problem resolution. Authors weave these elements together carefully, mindful that they interact in meaningful and engaging ways. Your analysis of an author's development of point of view could center on one or more of these elements. Specific genres within literature also have specific characteristics and features. For example, science fiction contains elements of the supernatural, while realistic fiction includes characters that are believable and events that could happen. Your analysis of an author's development of point of view could center on these features, too. Your ability to analyze these components of literature relies on your grade-level knowledge of literature basics.

Mark Twain (1835–1910) was the pen name of Samuel Clemens, author of numerous short stories and novels set in the American South, including *The Adventures of Tom Sawyer*, which was first published in 1876.

The passage in this chapter is an excerpt from the novel *The Adventures of Tom Sawyer* by Mark Twain. You'll be reading the passage and following an expert reader think through a sampling of the tips and tricks in the margin notes (feel free to refer back to the icon descriptors). It's as if you're tagging along with the expert reader.

The expert reader will then tackle some multiple-choice questions about the passages and a written response question. All of these activities help demonstrate how to apply these crucial skills to literature.

After this, it's your turn to practice. In chapter 3, you'll be reading a passage in which guided practice prompts cue your use of the tips and tricks for literature. You can check your thinking against possible responses.

An Excerpt from *The Adventures of Tom Sawyer*

by Mark Twain

Note to Reader: *The chapter opens as Tom is whitewashing a fence, a chore he was assigned by his Aunt Polly.*

But Tom's energy did not last. He began to think of the fun he had planned for this day, and his sorrows multiplied. Soon the free boys would come tripping along on all sorts of delicious expeditions, and they would make a world of fun of him for having to work—the very thought of it burnt him like fire. He got out his worldly wealth and examined it—bits of toys, marbles, and trash; enough to buy an exchange of *work*, maybe, but not half enough to buy

EXPERT READER:

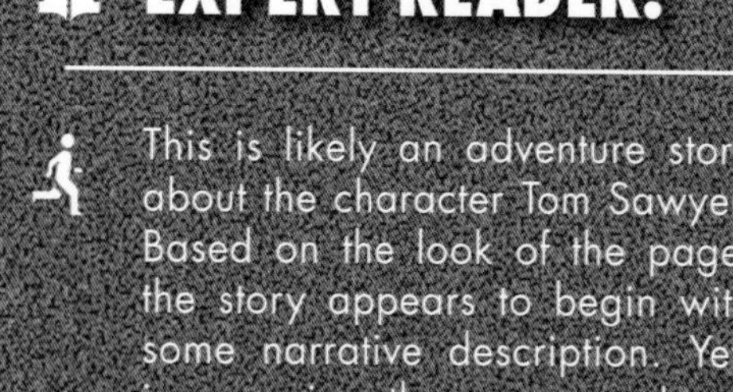
This is likely an adventure story about the character Tom Sawyer. Based on the look of the page, the story appears to begin with some narrative description. Yet, in scanning the passage, I see dialogue between characters is also used extensively. I'll have to determine who is telling the story.

From these few sentences, we quickly learn that Tom's anger is growing; he is mad about missing out on play because he must work instead, and he knows others will make fun of him. The problem is revealed.

so much as half an hour of pure freedom. So he returned his means to his pocket, and gave up the idea of trying to buy the boys. At this dark and hopeless moment an inspiration burst upon him! Nothing less than a great, magnificent inspiration.

He took up his brush and went tranquilly to work. Ben Rogers hove in sight presently—the very boy, of all boys, whose ridicule he had been dreading. He was eating an apple, and giving a long, melodious whoop, at intervals, followed by a deep-toned ding-dong-dong, for he was personating a steamboat. As he drew near, he slackened speed, took the middle of the street, leaned far over to starboard and rounded to with laborious pomp and circumstance—for he was personating the Big Missouri, and considered himself to be drawing nine feet of water. He was boat and captain and engine-bells combined, so he had to imagine himself standing on his own hurricane-deck giving the orders and executing them:

"Stop her, sir! Ting-a-ling-ling!" He drew up slowly toward the sidewalk.

"Ship up to back! Ting-a-ling-ling!" His arms stiffened down his sides.

"Stop the stabboard! Ting-a-ling-ling! Stop the labboard! Chow-ow-ow! Get out that head-line! *lively* now!

Tom went on whitewashing—paid no attention to the steamboat. Ben stared a moment and then said: *"Hi-Yi! You're* up a stump, ain't you!"

EXPERT READER:

A narrator who is not likely a character is telling the story and giving us full insights into Tom's actions and thoughts. I know that although Tom is angry, he has an idea as to how to solve this problem. The narrator calls the idea a "magnificent inspiration," and I am eager to learn about it.

We know that of all people to encounter, Ben is the "boy of all boys" Tom dreads. We expect ridicule and we expect to see Tom's idea begin to unfold.

EXPERT READER:

Despite the noise and clamor of the "Ting-a-lings," Tom intentionally ignores Ben. I know this because the narrator interjects a sentence describing Tom's actions. Tom's idea is likely unfolding, but I'm still unsure of his intentions—his response to a dreaded encounter is unusual and it makes me curious.

No answer. Tom surveyed his last touch with the eye of an artist, then he gave his brush another gentle sweep and surveyed the result, as before. Ben ranged up alongside of him. Tom's mouth watered for the apple, but he stuck to his work. Ben said:

Even though the narrator does not clue us in to Ben's thinking, we are clear about his intentions through his dialogue. We know he is sarcastic and that he is teasing Tom. Also, his taunts and ridicule confirm Tom's instincts. We trust Tom's ability to "read" people; he seems savvy.

"Hello, old chap, you got to work, hey?"

Tom wheeled suddenly and said:

"Why, it's you, Ben! I warn't noticing."

"Say—I'm going in a-swimming. Don't you wish you could? But of course you'd druther *work*—wouldn't you? Course you would!"

Tom contemplated the boy a bit, and said:

"What do you call work?"

"Why, ain't *that* work?"

Tom resumed his whitewashing, and answered carelessly:

"Well, maybe it is, and maybe it ain't. All I know, is, it suits Tom Sawyer."

"Oh come, now, you don't mean to let on that you *like* it?"

The brush continued to move.

I know for sure that Tom's plan is to dupe Ben. There's no way he truthfully considers the task of whitewashing a fence a rare opportunity.

"Like it? Well, I don't see why I oughtn't to like it. Does a boy get a chance to whitewash a fence every day?"

That put the thing in a new light. Tom swept his brush daintily back and forth—stepped back to note the effect—added a touch here and there—criticised the effect again—Ben watching every move and getting more interested, and more absorbed. Presently he said:

"Say, Tom, let *me* whitewash a little."

Tom considered, was about to consent; but he altered his mind:

"No—no—I reckon it wouldn't hardly do, Ben. You see, Aunt Polly's awful particular about this fence—but if it was the back fence I wouldn't mind and *she* wouldn't. Yes, she's awful particular about this fence; I reckon there ain't one boy in a thousand, maybe two thousand, that can do it the way it's got to be done."

"No—is that so? Oh come, now—lemme just try—I'd let *you*, if you was me, Tom."

"Ben, I'd like to, honest; but Aunt Polly—well, Jim wanted to do it, but she wouldn't let him; Sid wanted to do it, and she wouldn't let Sid. If you was to tackle this fence and anything was to happen to it— "

"Oh, shucks, I'll be just as careful. Now lemme try. Say—I'll give you the core of my apple."

"Well, here—No, Ben, now don't. I'm afeard—"

"I'll give you *all* of it!"

Tom gave up the brush with reluctance in his face, but alacrity in his heart. And while the late steamer Big Missouri worked and sweated in the sun, the retired artist sat on a barrel in the shade close by, munched his apple, and planned the slaughter of more innocents. Boys happened along every little while; they came

EXPERT READER:

The plot of this chapter is moving forward through the characters' rapid exchange of dialogue. I can see that Tom is baiting Ben. He discusses his finicky Aunt Polly and claims few boys are capable of the task. Meanwhile, the bait is too much for Ben to pass up.

EXPERT READER:

The narrator has returned to sum up the ending to Tom's plan. He uses figurative words, but I gather the gist is that Tom reveled in his trickery and conspired to trick more boys.

to jeer, but remained to whitewash. By the time Ben was tired out, Tom had traded the next chance to Billy Fisher for a kite, in good repair; and when he played out, Johnny Miller bought in for a dead rat and a string to swing it with—and so on, and so on. And when the middle of the afternoon came, from being a poor poverty-stricken boy in the morning, Tom was rolling in wealth. He had besides the things before mentioned, twelve marbles, a piece of blue bottle-glass to look through, a spool cannon, a fragment of chalk, a dog-collar—but no dog—the handle of a knife, and a dilapidated old window sash.

EXPERT READER:

This story is very carefully crafted. We learn about the characters through their actions, dialogue, and, in the case of Tom Sawyer, his thoughts, which are shared by a narrator. Some events unfold in front of us, while others are presented to us by the narrator.

He had had a nice, good, idle time all the while—plenty of company—and the fence had three coats of whitewash on it!

Tom said to himself that it was not such a hollow world, after all. He had discovered a great law of human action—namely, that in order to make a man or a boy covet a thing, it is only necessary to make the thing difficult to attain. If he had been a great and wise philosopher, like the writer of this book, he would now have comprehended that Work consists of whatever a body is *obliged* to do, and that Play consists of whatever a body is not obliged to do.

EXPERT READER:

It's interesting to note the tongue-in-cheek compliment the narrator pays to the author. Mark Twain playfully informs us of the story's lesson, a new discovery to a young boy, and a well-known lesson of life to a wise philosopher.

Samuel Clemens (aka Mark Twain) wrote a sequel to *The Adventures of Tom Sawyer,* which was titled *The Adventures of Huckleberry Finn.* Published in 1885, the work was considered by many literary critics to be "the Great American novel."

Mini Assessment

Now it's time to challenge your thinking by answering some multiple-choice questions and a written response question. Notice that more than one response to a multiple-choice question may seem correct. It's important to build evidence for the *best* answer. Carefully reviewing evidence by returning to the passage will be helpful.

1. How does the reader *primarily* learn Tom's true feelings in the story?

a) Through his conversations with the other character, Ben Rogers.

b) Through a third-person narrator, who informs the reader of Tom's thoughts.

c) Through Tom's actions, which reflect his true feelings.

d) Through Tom's Aunt Polly, who is particular about such things.

2. How is Ben's view of Tom's attitude toward his work different from the reader's view?

a) Ben believes Tom is letting on that he likes his work, while readers believe Tom thinks his work curbs his freedom.

b) Ben believes Tom finds his work worthwhile, and readers believe Tom finds his work enjoyable.

c) Ben believes Tom is letting on that he likes his work, while readers believe Tom finds his work enjoyable.

d) Ben believes Tom finds his work worthwhile, while readers believe Tom thinks his work curbs his freedom.

3. Closely reread the following sentence from the story: "Tom gave up the brush with reluctance in his face, but alacrity in his heart." What does this sentence mean?

a) Tom's expression showed he was unwilling to give up the brush, but deep down inside he was eager to hand it over.

b) Tom's expression showed he was very willing to give up the brush, but deep down inside he really wished to continue painting.
c) Tom's expression showed he was unwilling to give up the brush, but deep down inside he really wished to continue painting.
d) Tom had mixed feelings about turning over the brush and continuing to paint.

Check your answers. Were you correct?

1. b) is the best answer. We are informed of Tom's true feelings by the narrator in the chapter opening. We learn that Tom is sorrowful that he will miss out on expeditions the free boys have. He feels the situation is dark and hopeless until he becomes inspired by an idea.

2. d) is the best answer. Ben thinks that Tom enjoys painting, which is part of Tom's plan. Meanwhile, the reader is privy to the narrator's opening comments, which reflect Tom's true feelings—that he will miss out on the kinds of adventures the free boys will have.

3. a) is the best answer. From the start, Tom's interactions with Ben have been deceiving; his words and actions have not reflected his true thoughts or motives. Although I'm unsure of the meaning of the word "alacrity," I know that to say thoughts, actions, or words come from the heart generally implies they are truthful, and Tom truthfully wanted to get out of whitewashing the fence.

Expert Reader: I'm satisfied with my responses. In all cases, I returned to the text to check against evidence. At times, I had to dig deeply into the text and use clues and inferences while carefully weighing my thinking. I'm confident I can support my answers. I'm ready to try a short written response question.

Question: At the start of this chapter, a third-person narrator reveals Tom's feelings about having to whitewash the fence. What effect does this create for the reader as the story develops and ends? Use evidence from the text to support your answer.

Expert Reader Response

Through the insights provided by the narrator, readers are able to grasp Tom's plan to solve his problem. They also fully enjoy how Tom secretly executes it! From the start, readers are made aware by the narrator that Tom hates the idea of missing out on the fun he had planned because he must whitewash the fence. We know Tom feels hopeless and robbed of his freedom until he is inspired by a magnificent idea. Readers are curious to learn of his plan and soon understand that they are about to witness it through the action and dialogue that take place between Tom and Ben. In sum, readers watch and listen as Tom dupes Ben: "Tom surveyed his last touch with the eye of an artist, then he gave his brush another gentle sweep ..." The comedy of this action is clear only to the reader, who knows Tom's true feelings. The reader is even more amused when Ben falls for Tom's plan. "Lemme just try . . ." pleads Ben when Tom informs him that "there ain't one boy in a thousand . . . that can do it the way it's got to be done." In the end, the narrator reappears to inform the reader that Tom repeated this secret comedy over and over again. Not only did Tom get out of work, but he ended up with treasures. The narrator turns this chapter into a dramatic comedy purely for the reader's amusement.

Conclusion

How well do you feel you've grasped the expert reader's use of the tips and tricks for determining and assessing point of view and purpose? Decide if you're ready to move on to the guided practice in the next chapter or if you would like to take another pass through the expert reader's model.

CHAPTER 3

DETERMINING POINT OF VIEW AND PURPOSE IN LITERATURE: GUIDED PRACTICE

Directions: Now it's time for you to apply the tips and tricks during your close reading of a passage. The practice prompts icons will guide you (pages 9–11). Check to see if your responses to the prompts match possible responses provided.

Adapted from Chapter I, *The Time Machine* 

by H. G. Wells

The Time Traveler (so it will be convenient to speak of him) was explaining a very complicated matter to us as we sat before the blazing

GUIDED PRACTICE PROMPT:

What jump-start clues do you notice? Possible response: As I already know this is a passage of literature, I suspect the "time machine" could be a fictitious transportation vehicle. Perhaps this story is science fiction. Based on the "look" of the page, I can also tell a quick interchange of dialogue launches the story, suggesting that critical information is likely to be revealed in characters' conversations.

English novelist Herbert George Wells (1866–1946) is best remembered for his classic works in the genre of science fiction. *The Time Machine* and *The Invisible Man* are two of his well-known books.

fire, drinking wine and listening to his words.

"You must follow me carefully," he said. "I shall have to refute one or two ideas that are almost universally accepted."

"Is not that rather a large thing to expect us to begin upon?" said Filby, an argumentative man with red hair.

"I do not mean to ask you to accept anything without reasonable

GUIDED PRACTICE PROMPT:

Are you able to identify the point of view? Possible response: A character in the story is telling the story, although I don't know too much about him yet other than that he finds the Time Traveler's explanation to be complicated. So far, the story is unfolding in the first-person point of view.

ground for it," the Time Traveler said.

"Then continue," said the Psychologist.

"Clearly," the Time Traveler proceeded, "any object exists in four dimensions. It must have length, breadth, thickness – and duration."

"Yes, I understand," said the Very Young Man.

"The fourth dimension of duration," continued the Time Traveler, "is just another way of looking at time. Now, some philosophical people have been asking why we cannot move in time as we move in the other three dimensions. Surely you've heard their obscure views."

"I think so," murmured the Provincial Mayor, knitting his brows.

"But," said the Medical Man, "you cannot move at all in time! You cannot get away from the present moment."

The Time Traveler smiled. "My dear sir, that is just where you are wrong. This is the germ of my great discovery – that it is indeed possible to move along the time dimension."

"Surely that is against reason," said Filby.

The Time Traveler smiled. "Long ago," he said, "I had the vague inkling of a machine that could…"

"…travel through time?!" exclaimed the Very Young Man.

"Yes, and I have experimental verification."

Filby laughed.

GUIDED PRACTICE PROMPT:

Are you noticing the author's craft of text structure? Possible response: As I suspected, the plot begins to take shape as we follow the speaker recount a spirited discussion among many characters.

GUIDED PRACTICE PROMPT:

How can a breakdown of literary elements help? Possible response: Although the speaker does not provide us with a lot of information about the characters (other than that Filby is argumentative), the use of their role /position as designators (such as Psychologist, Young Man, Provincial Mayor, etc.) suggests the importance of their diverse roles over their identities. This must be intentional.

What are you thinking? Possible response: I can confirm that this is a time travel book, and I know Filby and the others are suspect of the Time Traveler's claims about the legitimacy of time travel.

GUIDED PRACTICE PROMPT:

Are you monitoring point of view? This is the first time the speaker has interjected his comments into the story. Although he, too, expresses disbelief, he questions the Time Traveler's "experimental verification." His response seems more sincere than the others', whose comments are disingenuous.

"It would be remarkably convenient for the historian," the Psychologist suggested. "One might travel back and verify the accepted account of the Battle of Hastings!"

"One might get one's Greek from the very lips of Homer and Plato," said the Very Young Man, "and then there is always the future! One might invest all one's money, leave it to accumulate at interest, and hurry on ahead."

"Experimental verification!" cried I. "You are going to verify *that*?"

"Let's see your experiment," challenged the Psychologist, "though it's all humbug, you know!"

The Time Traveler smiled round at us and he walked slowly out of the room, and we heard his slippers shuffling down the long passage to his laboratory.

The Psychologist looked at us. "I wonder what he's got?"

"Some sleight-of-hand trick or other," said the Medical Man.

The Time Traveler returned.

He was carrying a glittering metallic framework, scarcely larger than a small clock and very delicately made. There was ivory in it, and some transparent crystalline substance. And now I must be explicit, for this that follows – is an absolutely unaccountable thing. He placed the mechanism upon a table, then drew up a chair and sat down. We all watched, on the alert. It appears incredible to me that any kind of trick, however subtly conceived and however skillfully done, could have been played upon us under these conditions.

GUIDED PRACTICE PROMPT:

Are you monitoring point of view? Possible response: In this paragraph, the speaker addresses me, the reader, for the second time. Here, he claims that his description of events will be explicit because they are so unbelievable. He adds at the end that trickery was unlikely. He's pretty convincing.

How can a breakdown of literary elements help? Possible response: As the story continues to unfold, I'm feeling confident in my original thinking that time travel adventures will likely comprise the plot of this story. The "bigger machine" will transport the Time Traveler and probably some of the characters, including the speaker, to another time.

"This little affair," said the Time Traveler, "is only a model. It is the prototype for a bigger machine." The Medical Man got up out of his chair and peered into the thing. Then, after we had all imitated the action of the Medical Man, the Time Traveler said, "Now this little lever," indicating a rod of ivory, "sends the machine gliding into the future, and this one sends it back in time. I am going to move this lever, and off the machine will go. It will pass into the future time and disappear. Have a good look at the thing. Satisfy yourself there is no trickery. I don't want to waste this model, and then be told I'm a quack."

The Time Traveler moved his hand towards the lever, and then suddenly turned to the Psychologist. "No. Lend me your hand." He took the man's hand and pressed the lever forward.

We all saw the lever move. There was a breath of wind, and one of the candles on the mantelpiece was blown out. The little machine on the table swung around, became faint . . . and vanished!

Everyone was silent for a moment. The Psychologist looked under the table. The Time Traveler laughed.

How can text structure help you here? Possible response: This event marks a turning point in this chapter as the Time Traveler is now laughing at his guests' reactions. Earlier, Filby laughed at the Time Traveler's claim of experimental verification of the existence of time travel.

"Look here," said the Medical Man, "are you in earnest about this? Do you seriously believe that the machine has traveled in time?"

Published in 1895, *The Time Machine* was adapted into a 1960 science fiction film starring Rod Taylor, Yvette Mimieux, and Alan Young. The film received an Oscar for time-lapse photographic effects showing the world changing rapidly.

"Certainly," replied the Time Traveler, filling his pipe. "I have a much bigger machine nearly finished in my laboratory. And soon I intend to travel upon it. Would you care to see the time itself?"

I remember vividly the flickering light, how we all followed him, puzzled but incredulous, and how there in the laboratory we beheld a larger edition of the little mechanism which we had seen vanish from before our eyes.

"Look here," said the Medical Man, "are you perfectly serious?"

"Upon that machine," said the Time Traveler, "I intend to explore time. I was never more serious in my life."

None of us quite knew how to take it.

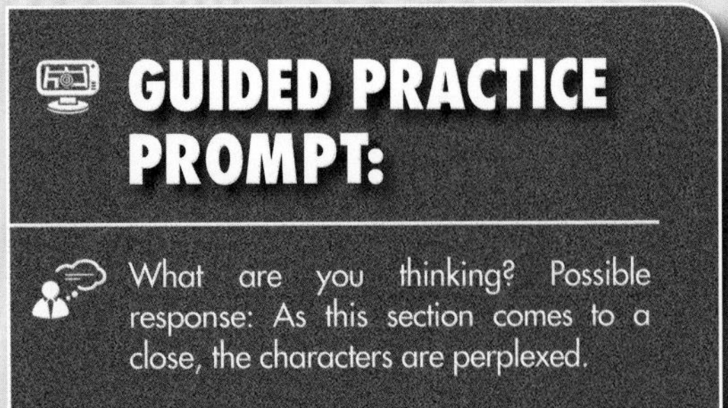

I caught Filby's eye over the shoulder of the Medical Man, and he winked at me solemnly.

At this point, you should be able to apply the tips and tricks for determining and assessing point of view and purpose. Challenge yourself by answering some multiple-choice questions and a written response question.

Mini Assessment

Remember that it's important to use evidence to build a case for the *best* answer. Return to the text to gauge which response is best supported.

1. How does the reader *primarily* learn about the characters in this story?

a) The Time Traveler asks them to share their views.
b) The narrator identifies them by occupation and recounts their words and actions.
c) Filby's arguments cause them to lighten the mood by joking.
d) Readers rely on their background knowledge.

2. If Filby were the narrator, how might this passage be different?

a) Filby would dispute the Time Traveler's ideas and call him a quack.

b) Filby would agree with the Provincial Mayor and express uncertainty about scientific matters.

c) Filby would agree with the Young Man and invest his money to accumulate interest.

d) Filby would admit that time travel was possible after seeing the time machine.

3. Closely reread this sentence from the passage: "Experimental verification!" cried I. "You are going to verify *that*?" What effect does this have in the story's development?

a) The speaker is curious about the Time Traveler's evidence as he hopes to travel in time.

b) The speaker is certain the Time Traveler has proof and hopes the evidence will convince the other guests.

c) The speaker is certain the Time Traveler does not have proof and hopes to disprove the idea of time travel.

d) The speaker is curious about the Time Traveler's evidence, suggesting he may believe in time travel.

Check your answers against an expert reader's. Were you correct?

1. b) is the best answer. The story is told from the narrator's point of view. The narrator informs the reader of the events that took place, including the guests' dialogue. Through these, the readers learn about the characters.

2. a) is the best answer. Filby is argumentative and opinionated. He remains doubtful about the legitimacy of the Time Traveler. It's unlikely he would change his mind.

3. d) is the best answer. Unlike the other guests, the narrator doesn't ridicule the Time Traveler's claim. His curiosity is sincere. This suggests he may believe the Time Traveler.

Expert Reader: Is your understanding and analysis of the passage taking shape? Did you return to the passage and find evidence to support your responses? Did your answer square with the evidence? Are you comfortable discussing or writing a response to the following written response question? Either talk through your answer or jot it down on a separate piece of paper.

Question: As we read science fiction, we are asked to suspend our disbelief about fictitious or supernatural events that take place so that we enjoy the story as it unfolds. Explain how the author uses point of view in this story to encourage readers to do this.

Expert Reader Response

In this passage, readers are able to suspend their disbelief about the possibility of time travel (and what might follow) largely as a result of the point of view that is used within the story. From the start, readers recognize that the unnamed storyteller is a character in the story; he recounts the events and discussions of the Time Traveler's guests and also interjects his own views into the discussions. As the Time Traveler attempts to verify the possibility of time travel, the speaker makes us aware of the array of objections and ridicule expressed by the other characters (which we may initially share). He does this by recounting their dialogue and their actions: "'One might get one's Greek from the very lips of Homer and Plato,'" said the Very Young Man.'" Even the speaker expresses his own disbelief: "'Experimental verification!" cried I. "'You are going to verify that?'" We are in full agreement with the disbelieving speaker and, over time, come to trust him. It's no wonder that as he begins to waiver about the possibility of time travel, we, too, are able to temporarily suspend our disbelief for the purpose of enjoying the story as it unfolds. "'And now I must be explicit, for this that follows – is an absolutely unaccountable thing.'"

We heed his warning yet are ready to let go of our disbelief, just as he has.

Conclusion

How well have you grasped the tips and trick for determining and assessing point of view and purpose in literature? Based on your performance and self-evaluations, decide if you've mastered the skills or if you would like to take another pass through this guided practice before moving on to the next chapter.

CHAPTER 4

DETERMINING POINT OF VIEW AND PURPOSE IN INFORMATIONAL TEXT: EXPERT READER MODEL

Now let's see how to apply the tips and tricks to informational text. Informational text is a type of nonfiction, or factual text, that is written to inform the reader, explain something, or convey information about the natural and social worlds. Informational text can include newspaper articles, magazine articles, autobiographies, speeches, opinion pieces, editorials, and historical, scientific, technical, or economic accounts.

Authors of informational text have a point to make about a topic. They frequently want to change your thinking in some way or add to your understanding. One way authors do this is by purposefully choosing a particular point of view in which to present information. This point of view develops and shapes the content and style of the text. Awareness of point of view helps a reader evaluate ideas and improves comprehension of text.

Plan of Action

The passage in this chapter is an excerpt from *Theodore Roosevelt, An Autobiography*. Similar to chapter 2, you'll be reading the excerpt while following an expert reader think through the tips and tricks—this time as they are applied to informational text. You may want to refresh your memory by reviewing the tips and tricks before beginning.

Again, you'll *observe* the expert reader work through some multiple-choice questions and a written response question to get the full impact of how to determine and assess point of view and purpose in informational text.

Then, in the chapter that follows, it will be your turn to practice. You'll start by reading a passage in which guided practice prompts and icons cue your use of the tips and tricks. You can check your thinking against possible responses.

I know autobiographies are life stories written by the person who actually lived the life. I also know that it's difficult to be entirely objective when writing about your own life. Although I'll see the world from Theodore Roosevelt's perspective, I'll need to ask myself if I'm getting an honest re-creation of events.

Excerpt from: *Theodore Roosevelt, An Autobiography*

by Theodore Roosevelt

(Theodore Roosevelt was the twenty-sixth president of the United States. He is noted for his exuberant personality and "cowboy" persona, his range of interests and achievements, and his leadership of the Progressive Movement.)

Having been a sickly boy, with no natural bodily prowess, and having lived much at home, I was at first quite unable to hold my own when thrown into contact with other boys of rougher antecedents.

Theodore Roosevelt (1858–1919), the twenty-sixth president of the United States, was well known for his exuberant personality.

I was nervous and timid. Yet from reading of the people I admired—ranging from the soldiers of Valley Forge, and Morgan's riflemen, to the heroes of my favorite stories—and from hearing of the feats performed by my Southern forefathers and kinsfolk, and from knowing my father, I felt a great admiration for men who were fearless and who could hold their own in the world, and I had a great desire to be like them. Until I was nearly fourteen I let this desire take no more definite shape than day-dreams. Then an incident happened that did me real good. Having an attack of asthma, I was sent off by myself to Moosehead Lake. On the stage-coach ride thither I encountered a couple of other boys who were about my own age, but very much more competent and also much more mischievous. I have no doubt they were good-hearted boys, but they were boys! They found that I was a foreordained and predestined victim, and industriously proceeded to make life miserable for me.

The experience taught me what probably no amount of good advice could have taught me. I made up my mind that I must try to learn so that I would not again be put in such a helpless position; and having become quickly and bitterly conscious that I did not have the natural prowess to hold my own, I decided that I would try to supply its place by training. Accordingly, with my father's hearty approval,

EXPERT READER:

This is very interesting, but it doesn't seem to match the public persona of Theodore Roosevelt that I'm familiar with, of him being outgoing and fearless.

I can infer that Roosevelt may have led a sheltered childhood due to illness but that he was an avid reader with a vivid imagination, which led to the development of strong role models.

I know authors use ancedotes to establish connections between ideas and events. I can assume that Roosevelt included this story to show why and how he learned to protect himself outside of his daydreams.

I started to learn to box. I was a painfully slow and awkward pupil, and certainly worked two or three years before I made any perceptible improvement whatever. I did a good deal of boxing and wrestling in Harvard, but never attained to the first rank in either, even at my own weight. The chief part I played was to act as trial horse for some friend or classmate who did have a chance of distinguishing himself in the championship contests. 

• • • •

There are two kinds of success, or, rather, two kinds of ability displayed in the achievement of success. There is, first, the success either in big things or small things which comes to the man who has in him the natural power to do what no one else can do, and what no amount of training, no perseverance or will power, will enable any ordinary man to do. This is the most striking kind of success, and it can be attained only by the man who has in him the quality which separates him in kind no less than in degree from his fellows. But much the commoner type of success in every walk of life and in every species of effort is that which comes to the man who differs from his fellows not by the kind of quality which he possesses but by the degree of development which he has given that quality. This kind of success is open to a large number of persons, if only they seriously

EXPERT READER:

This is a clear example of cause and effect text structure. Also, I can't help but think that this small story will continue to be important throughout Roosevelt's life, since he is remembered as being the very opposite of timid and nervous. How did he become so fearless? Was this the "jumping off" point for him?

So, boxing was not something that Roosevelt was naturally good at or excelled at. Yet, he did not give up and continued boxing when he was in college. He even shows some humor by saying he was basically a sparring practice partner for other, more accomplished boxers. I'm thinking this is probably an accurate and honest reflection on Roosevelt's part.

Based on the boxing story, this first type of success doesn't sound like the kind of success Roosevelt was familiar with!

EXPERT READER:

I can now understand why Roosevelt shared the bullying and boxing stories. He's trying to show us that through his experiences, he developed the perspective that anyone can overcome adversity with determination.

Theodore Roosevelt wanted to persuade the reader to believe in the power of hard work and determination and the resulting success. He wants us to see that he knows from experience that we all have the power of success within us, although it won't come easy for most of us. Rather, most success takes hard work and perseverance.

This seems to be an honest reflection on Theodore Roosevelt's part. Based on his life experiences, I believe his point of view concerning life is if we work hard and make good decisions when given the opportunity, we can find whatever success we are looking for.

determine to achieve it. It is the kind of success which is open to the average man of sound body and fair mind, who has no remarkable mental or physical attributes, but who gets just as much as possible in the way of work out of the aptitudes that he does possess. It is the only kind of success that is open to most of us. Yet some of the greatest successes in history have been those of this second class—when I call it second class I am not running it down in the least, I am merely pointing out that it differs in kind from the first class. To the average man it is probably more useful to study this second type of success than to study the first. From the study of the first he can learn inspiration, he can get uplift and lofty enthusiasm. From the study of the second he can, if he chooses, find out how to win a similar success himself.

I need hardly say that all the successes I have ever won have been of the second type. I never won anything without hard labor and the exercise of my best judgment and careful planning and working long in advance. Having been a rather sickly and awkward boy, I was as a young man at first both nervous and distrustful of my own prowess. I had to train myself painfully and laboriously not merely as regards my body but as regards my soul and spirit.

Mini Assessment

Now it's time to challenge your thinking by answering some multiple-choice questions and a written response question. Notice that in some multiple-choice questions, more than one answer may be considered correct. It is important to use evidence to build a case for the *best* answer. Carefully reviewing evidence by returning to the passage will be helpful. Gauging which response is best supported through the evidence is critical.

1. Which sentence from the passage *best* conveys Theodore Roosevelt's point of view about role models?

a) Role models lead to daydreaming.
b) Role models can have a positive, guiding effect.
c) Role models can have a negative, guiding effect.
d) Good role models are based on characters from literature.

2. Based on the information presented in this excerpt, why did Roosevelt *most likely* choose to write about his boxing experiences in college?

a) To persuade readers to see that you don't have to be the best at something for it to be valuable.
b) To make the argument that boxing is the best sport to pursue if you want to be successful.
c) To entertain readers by describing his personal experiences while in college at Harvard.
d) To inform the reader that boxing is a difficult sport to be good at.

3. How does the speaker, Theodore Roosevelt, convey his *main* purpose in this excerpt?

a) By retelling the story of how he was bullied as a boy, he conveys sympathy for victims of bullying.

b) By describing the men he considered to be heroes, he imparts knowledge to readers.
c) By describing his efforts to learn how to box, he inspires others to work long and hard to reach a goal.
d) By telling about people with natural physical abilities, he imparts his dislike for them.

Check your answers. Were you correct?

1. b) is the best answer. Much of the text in the first paragraph works as evidence to prove that Theodore Roosevelt admired people who were fearless and who could hold their own in the world. After the bullying incident, he decided to make purposeful decisions that would help guide him in having these character traits as well.

2. a) is the best answer. Roosevelt uses his experience of being an average boxer to explain that even though he "never attained to the first rank" or was the best, the actual experience of learning to box helped him attain his goal of being fearless and able to take care of himself. Even if he didn't win contests, he still knew how to box if the need arose and he needed to defend himself.

3. c) is the best answer. Roosevelt's goal was to be like his role models; fearless and able to take care of himself. After being bullied, he decided that boxing was the path he would pursue to begin achieving this goal. He describes himself as a "painfully slow and awkward pupil" and includes the detail that it took "two to three years before he made any perceptible improvement whatever" to inspire others to work toward their goals, no matter how difficult and slow the progress may seem. Roosevelt ultimately became known for his fearless "cowboy" persona.

Expert Reader: I'm satisfied with my responses. In all cases, I returned to the text to check against evidence. At times, I had to dig deeply

By his own admission, Theodore Roosevelt was a nervous and timid boy until an encounter with a group of boys convinced him to learn to box as a way to "hold his own."

into the text and use clues and inferences while carefully weighing my thinking. I'm confident I can argue in support of my answers with credible evidence from the text.

Question: What did Theodore Roosevelt hope to achieve in this excerpt from *Theodore Roosevelt, An Autobiography*? Use evidence from the text to support your answer.

Expert Reader Response

Theodore Roosevelt wanted readers to understand that success is attainable for every person, but only if they are willing to plan ahead, work hard and long, and make good decisions. By using examples from his childhood, Roosevelt shows us how important it is to have a goal and then take steps to achieve that goal. For instance, from the time he was a boy, Roosevelt knew he wanted to be fearless and to be able to hold his own in the world, just like his role models. After he was bullied on a stagecoach ride, he realized that just wanting something was not enough. He would actually need to take purposeful action, so he made the decision to learn how to box. Although Roosevelt shares that he was never actually very good at boxing, the experience of learning and practicing gave him the foundation he needed eventually to be successful as the twenty-sixth president of the United States.

Conclusion

How well do you feel you've grasped the expert reader's use of tips and tricks for determining and assessing point of view and purpose? Decide if you're ready to move on to the guided practice in the next chapter or if you would like to take another pass through the expert reader's model.

CHAPTER 5

DETERMINING POINT OF VIEW AND PURPOSE IN INFORMATIONAL TEXT: GUIDED PRACTICE

Next, it's time for you to apply the tips and tricks during your close reading of a passage. The practice prompt icons will guide you. Check to see if your responses to the prompts match the possible responses provided.

An Excerpt from: *Editorials from the Hearst Newspapers*

by Arthur Brisbane

(Arthur Brisbane (1864–1936) was one of the best-known American newspaper editors of the twentieth century. In 1882, he began work as a newspaper reporter and eventually became the editor of the New York Journal. *His syndicated editorial column had an estimated daily readership of more than twenty million.)*

GUIDED PRACTICE PROMPT:

How can jump-start clues help you? Possible response: I know editorials are opinion writing pieces. Opinions are views or judgments not necessarily based on fact. As a reader, I'll need to evaluate the accuracy and logic of the points being made.

Arthur Brisbane (1864–1936) wrote a syndicated editorial column called "Today" from 1917 to 1936.

Your Work Is Your Brain's Gymnasium?

For "buyers" in big stores,

For clerks in little stores,

For office boys,

For typewriters, reporters, car conductors, household domestics, for all who are hired to work for others, this article is intended.

There is no greater mistake than skimping on our work—BECAUSE YOU ARE WORKING FOR ANOTHER, AND FEAR YOU MAY DO TOO MUCH.

For your own sake remember that whatever you do in the way of honest concentrated work you do FIRST OF ALL FOR YOURSELF.

Only one thing in the world can improve you and better your condition, and that thing is your own effort. You begin life with certain mental faculties, and with certain muscular faculties. Their development or decay depends entirely on yourself.

No work that you do is worthless. It will NEVER pay you to neglect or slur the task that you have undertaken. You may be idle, in the thought that you are indulging yourself at the expense of your employer. It is a dishonest thought, and it is a stupid thought at the same time. You may rob your employer

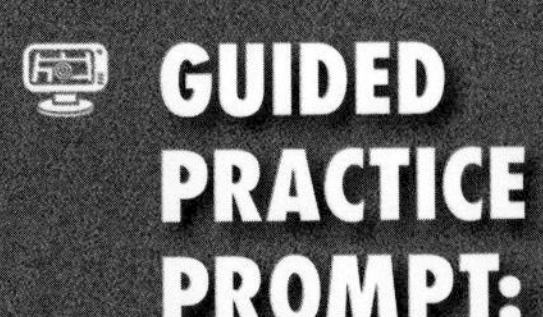

GUIDED PRACTICE PROMPT:

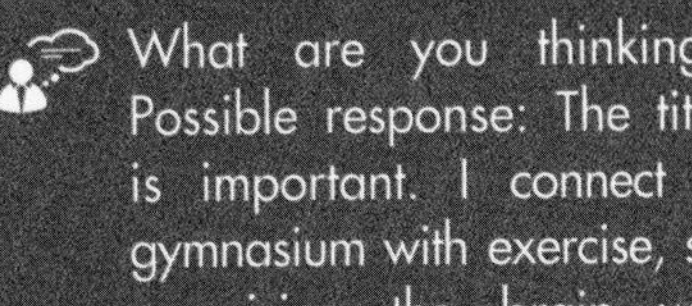

What are you thinking? Possible response: The title is important. I connect a gymnasium with exercise, so exercising the brain will most likely be discussed.

Are you noticing the author's craft and/or text structure? Possible response: The author has identified the audience for which this editorial is written—all people who are hired to work for others.

Can you identify the author's point of view or perspective? Possible response: These paragraphs clearly state the author's perspective on work: Do whatever work you do to the best of your ability, not for your employer, but for your own satisfaction and growth.

GUIDED PRACTICE PROMPT:

What are you thinking? Possible response: What does the author want me to know after reading these paragraphs? I think he's saying that while I may be fooling my employer by not working up to par, I'm hurting myself morally because I'll know I was paid for work I didn't perform.

of the time that he pays for, but when you shirk your work you rob yourself first of all.----

You may say that your employer pays too little. Perhaps he does. But that is no reason for hurting your moral character through dishonesty. It is no excuse for failing to develop yourself.

The store, or factory, or office in which you work is to your mind what a gymnasium is to your muscles.

You enter a gymnasium AND PAY FOR THE PRIVILEGE OF WORKING THERE. You do not say to yourself: "This gymnasium belongs to another man. The profits go to him, and so I'll not work hard." On the contrary, you realize that the owner of the gymnasium gives you the chance to develop your muscles and you thank him, although he makes you pay for the privilege. And you do your very best, on the trapeze, rings, parallel bars, or in any other direction.

GUIDED PRACTICE PROMPT:

How can a breakdown of literary elements help? Possible response: I know authors use examples and comparisons to help establish relationships between ideas and to shape a reader's thinking. Here, the author compares the workplace to a gymnasium and basically says a worker should thank the employer for the opportunity to think and develop his or her brain.

ACT IN YOUR WORK AS YOU DO IN YOUR GYMNASIUM HOURS.

There is no kind of work that can fail to make you a better and more successful man if you work at it honestly and loyally. If you sweep an office, sweep it well. And begin punctually each day, remembering that punctuality acquired in sweeping an office may be used later in governing a city.

Train your mind through your work, whatever it is. Study the lives of those who have succeeded. You will see that they did whatever they did as well as they could.

Edison was an ordinary telegraph operator. But he was not content with merely working as others worked. He worked very hard, devised means to make more valuable the instruments of his employers. Soon he was an employer himself, and what is far better than being an employer, he was a creator of new ideas and a benefactor of the world.

GUIDED PRACTICE PROMPT:

Can you identify the author's point of view or perspective? Possible response: I think the author is saying that what you do today can help you tomorrow in ways you might not immediately be able to see.

How can a breakdown of literary elements help? Possible response: Here is another example to give credibility to the author's perspective that what you do today can help you tomorrow. What Edison learned from his work for his employers, he used to create new ideas and start his own business.

MERELY WORKING "FAIRLY WELL" IS NOT ENOUGH.

If you want to run a mile fast, you do not merely jog. You try every day to run the mile faster than you did the day before. If you want to learn to jump high, you strain your muscles and try over and over to do what you can't do. Ultimately, you achieve it. Keep that in mind when you work. Remember that you must wind yourself up. The most watchful employer may discharge you. But he cannot wind you up. Be a self-winding machine, and keep yourself wound up.

GUIDED PRACTICE PROMPT:

Are you noticing the author's craft and/or text structure? Possible response: The author uses examples and comparisons to guide me to a central idea: Just as we are self-motivated to excel in physical activities, we need to be self-motivated to excel in mental activities.

Arthur Brisbane's editorial column had an estimated daily readership of more than twenty million.

Your hardest effort may fail to achieve greatness. But honest work will at least make it impossible for you to be a failure. Train your brain, nerves and muscles to regular, steady, conscientious effort. Make up your mind that FOR YOUR OWN SAKE you will make every effort your best effort. You will soon find yourself a more successful, more self-respecting, abler man or woman. 

And here is an argument that should be more powerful with you than self-interest: Remember that that world needs honest, conscientious men and women, able to do good work themselves. Make up your mind to be one of the world's HONEST citizens.

To improve the world begin by improving yourself. 

GUIDED PRACTICE PROMPT:

What are you thinking? Possible response: Phrases like "impossible ... to be a failure" and "for your own sake" help me infer that the author believes that you should find satisfaction in the fact that you've done your best, regardless of the end result.

Can you identify the author's point of view or perspective? Possible response: I think the final point of view the author leaves us with is also the central idea of this editorial: Through self-motivation and hard work, we improve ourselves and in turn, improve the world around us. This seems like pretty sound advice.

At this point, you should be able to apply the tips and tricks for determining and assessing point of view and purpose and challenge yourself by answering some multiple-choice questions and a written response question.

Mini Assessment

Again, be aware that it is important to use evidence to build a case for the *best* answer. Remember to review evidence carefully by returning to the passage to gauge which response is best supported.

1. What is the author's *main* purpose for including the paragraph describing Thomas Edison?

a) To explain how Edison began work as a telegraph operator.

b) To describe the instruments Edison worked on.
c) To illustrate how hard work can lead to other opportunities.
d) To show that being an employer is better than being an employee.

2. Which sentence *best* describes the author's point of view and the kinds of details used to support it in the passage?

a) The writer is negative and provides details about how difficult it is to work for another person.
b) The writer is positive and includes details that show the effects of self-motivation.
c) The writer is neutral and provides facts without any statements of opinion about how work improves moral character.
d) The writer is doubtful and provides details showing that exercise will probably not improve a person's life.

3. With which statement would Arthur Brisbane *most likely* agree?

a) If everyone would work hard, they would be happier.
b) Being an employer is better than working for an employer.
c) The first step to being successful is working out.
d) Success is determined by the way work is done.

Check your answers against an expert reader's. Were you correct?

1. c) is the best answer. The story of Edison's success illustrates, or gives a concrete example that makes an idea easier to understand, Brisbane's view that as you learn from one job, you prepare yourself for another. Edison's story validates Brisbane's claim.

2. b) is the best answer. When Brisbane speaks of being "a self-winding machine and keeping yourself wound up," we can infer

Authors of informational text purposefully choose a particular point of view in which to present information that they hope will add to a reader's understanding of the topic.

that he is speaking of being self-motivated or possessing an internal drive to get something accomplished. He connects being self-motivated with positive effects of being "more successful, more self-respecting" and an "abler man or woman" in the paragraph that follows.

3. d) is the best answer. Throughout the entire editorial, Brisbane expresses his point of view on how work should be performed. He advises against skimping on our work and explains that being idle at work is a dishonest practice. When we are dishonest, our moral character is affected. He further advises that honest work makes it "impossible for you to be a failure" and that when best effort is put forward, you will "soon find yourself more successful."

Expert Reader: Is your understanding and analysis of the passage taking shape? Did you return to the passage and find evidence to support your responses? Did your answers square with the evidence? Are you comfortable discussing or writing a response to the following written response question? Again, either talk through your answer or jot it down on a separate piece of paper.

Question: What was Arthur Brisbane's purpose for writing this editorial? Use evidence from the text to support your answer.

Expert Reader Response

Arthur Brisbane wrote this editorial to express his point of view that the only way to improve ourselves and others around us is through our own effort. He uses many examples of work to illustrate this. For example, Brisbane suggests that when we are idle at our job, no matter what that job is, we are choosing to be dishonest, which doesn't help us at all. In fact, it hurts our moral character. Brisbane further argues that when we are honest citizens, we improve ourselves and the rest of the world. He also uses a story about Thomas Edison to illustrate his point. Edison used what he learned working as a telegraph operator to improve the instruments used to communicate. His work allowed him to become his own employer, but, more importantly, he became a benefactor of the world. This means he helped not only himself, but many others.

Conclusion

How well have you grasped the tips and tricks for determining and assessing point of view and purpose in informational text? Based on your performance and self-evaluations, decide if you've mastered the skills or if you would like to take another pass through this guided practice. Congratulations if you're ready to move on!

A New Expert Reader!

Now that you've mastered how to use the tips and tricks for determining and assessing point of view and purpose, you're on your way to becoming an expert reader! Continue to practice with different types of literature and informational text. You'll see that your attempts to grapple with classroom and assigned tasks are far easier now.

GLOSSARY

ANALYZE To carefully examine, inspect, and consider a text in order to fully understand it.

ASSESS To evaluate, determine, judge, or appraise.

AUTOBIOGRAPHY An account of a person's life written by that person.

CENTRAL IDEA The key concept or message being expressed.

CLOSE READING The deep, analytical reading of a brief passage of text in which the reader constructs meaning based on author intention and text evidence. The close reading of a text enables readers to gain insights that exceed a cursory reading.

DIALOGUE Words spoken by characters in a story, play, etc., usually set off with quotation marks in text.

DISTRACTOR Anything that steers a reader away from the text evidence and weakens or misguides analysis.

EDITORIAL A newspaper article written by an editor that gives an opinion on a topical issue.

EVIDENCE Information from the text that a reader uses to prove a position, conclusion, inference, or big idea.

FIRST PERSON POINT OF VIEW Use of a narrator who is a character in the story.

FIX-UP STRATEGY Common technique used when meaning is lost.

GENRE A system used to classify types or kinds of writing.

INFERENCE A conclusion that a reader draws about something by using information that is available.

INFORMATIONAL TEXT A type of nonfiction text, such as an article, essay, opinion piece, memoir, or historical, scientific, technical, or economic account, which is written to give facts or inform about a topic.

LITERARY ELEMENTS A component part found in a whole work of literature.

LITERATURE Imaginary writing, such as poetry, mysteries, myths, creation stories, science fiction, allegories and other genres that tell a story.

NARRATOR The teller of the story in a text.

PERSPECTIVE The angle from which a story is told or from which information is presented.

PERSUASIVE TEXT Nonfiction text intended to convince the reader of the validity of a set of ideas.

POINT OF VIEW The perspective, or position, from which the story is told.

SPECIAL EFFECTS Suspense or humor are two examples of special effects that may be created through point of view.

TEXT FEATURE One of a variety of tools used to organize text and to give readers more information about the text.

TEXT STRUCTURE the logical arrangement and organization of ideas in a text using sentences, lines, paragraphs, stanzas, sections, etc.

THEME The central message of a text or what the story is really about.

THIRD PERSON POINT OF VIEW Use of a narrator who is not a character in the story.

FOR MORE INFORMATION

Council of Chief State School Officers
One Massachusetts Avenue, NW
Suite 700
Washington, DC 20001-1431
(202) 336-7000
Website: http://www.ccsso.org
The Common Core State Standards Initiative is a state-led effort coordinated by the National Governors Association Center for Best Practices (NGA Center) and the Council of Chief State School Officers (CCSSO). The standards provide a clear and consistent framework to prepare students for college and the workforce.

National Association for the Education of Young Children
1313 L Street NW, Suite 500
Washington, DC 20005
(202) 232-8777
Website: http://www.naeyc.org
The National Association for the Education of Young Children is the world's largest organization working on behalf of young children.

National Education Association
1201 16th Street NW
Washington, DC 20036-3290
(202) 833-4000
Website: http://www.nea.org
The National Education Association (NEA), the nation's largest professional employee organization, is committed to advancing the cause of public education.

National Governors Association
Hall of the States
444 North Capitol Street, Suite 267
Washington, DC 20001-1512
(202) 624-5300
Website: http://www.nga.org
The National Governors Association and the Council of Chief State School Officers go together—both organizations were responsible for the creation of the Common Core State Standards so they share the description provided.

National Parent Teacher Association
12250 North Pitt Street
Alexandria, VA 22314
(703) 518-1200
Website: http://www.pta.org
National PTA enthusiastically supports the adoption and implementation by all states of the Common Core State Standards. The standards form a solid foundation for high-quality education.

New York State Education Department
89 Washington Avenue
Albany, NY 12234
(518) 474-3852
Website: http://www.engageny.org
EngageNY.org is developed and maintained by the New York State Education Department. This is the official website for current materials and resources related to the implementation of the New York State pre-K–12 Common Core Learning Standards (CCLS).

Partnership for Assessment of Readiness for College and Careers
1400 16th Street NW, Suite 510
Washington, DC 20036
(202) 745-2311
Website: http://www.parcconline.org

The Partnership for Assessment of Readiness for College and Careers (PARCC) is a consortium of eighteen states plus the District of Columbia and the U.S. Virgin Islands working together to develop a common set of K–12 assessments in English and math anchored in what it takes to be ready for college and careers.

The Smarter Balanced Assessment Consortium
Old Capitol Building
P.O. Box 47200
600 Washington Street SE
Olympia, WA 98504-7200
(360) 725-6000
Website: http://www.smarterbalanced.org

The Smarter Balanced Assessment Consortium is developing a system of valid, reliable, and fair next-generation assessments aligned to the Common Core State Standards (CCSS) in English language arts/literacy (ELA/literacy) and mathematics for grades 3–8 and 11. The system includes summative and formative assessments to provide meaningful feedback to help students succeed.

U.S. Department of Education
Department of Education Building
400 Maryland Avenue SW
Washington, DC 20202

(800) 872-5327
Website: http://www.ed.gov
Nearly every state has now adopted the Common Core State Standards. The federal government has supported this state-led effort by helping ensure that higher standards are being implemented for all students and that educators are being supported in transitioning to new standards.

Websites

Due to the changing nature of Internet links, Rosen Publishing has developed an online list of Web sites related to the subject of this book. This site is updated regularly. Please use this link to access the list:

http://www.rosenlinks.com/CCRGR/POV

BIBLIOGRAPHY

Beers, Kylene, and Robert E. Probst. *Notice & Note: Strategies for Close Reading*. Portsmouth, NH: Heinemann, 2013.

Brisbane, Arthur. *Editorials from the Hearst Newspapers*. Albertson Publishing Co., 1906. (Public Domain.)

Fountas, Irene C., and Gay Su Pinnell. *Genre Prompting Guide for Fiction.* Portsmouth, NH: Heinemann, 2012.

Fountas, Irene C., and Gay Su Pinnell. *Genre Prompting Guide for Nonfiction, Poetry, and Test Taking*. Portsmouth, NH: Heinemann, 2012.

Fountas, Irene C., and Gay Su Pinnell. *Genre Quick Guide, Grades K - 8+*. Portsmouth, NH: Heinemann, 2012.

Fountas, Irene C., and Gay Su Pinnell. *Genre Study: Teaching with Fiction and Nonfiction Books*. Portsmouth, NH: Heinemann, 2012.

Roosevelt, Theodore. *Theodore Roosevelt, An Autobiography*. Charles Scribner's Sons, 1920. (Public Domain.)

Twain, Mark (Samuel Clemens). *The Adventures of Tom Sawyer*. The American Publishing Company, 1884. (Public Domain.)

Wells, H. G. (Herbert George). *The Time Machine*. Heinemann, 1895. (Public Domain.)

INDEX

About the Authors

Sandra K. Athans is a national board-certified practicing classroom teacher with fifteen years of experience teaching reading and writing at the elementary level. She is the author of several teacher-practitioner books on literacy including *Quality Comprehension* and *Fun-tastic Activities for Differentiating Comprehension Instruction*, both published by the International Reading Association. Athans has presented her research at the International Reading Association, the National Council of Teachers of English Conferences, and the New York State Reading Association Conferences. Her contributions have appeared in well-known literacy works including *The Literacy Leadership Handbook* and *Strategic Writing Mini-Lessons*. She is also a children's book writer and specializes in high-interest, photo-informational books published with Millbrook Press, a division of Lerner Publishing Group.

Athans earned a BA in English from the University of Michigan, an MA in elementary education from Manhattanville College, and an MS in literacy (birth–grade 6) from Le Moyne College. She is also certified to teach secondary English. In addition to teaching in an elementary classroom, she is an adjunct professor at Le Moyne College and provides instruction in graduate-level literacy classes. This spring she was named Outstanding Elementary Social Studies Educator by the Central New York Council for the Social Studies. Athans serves on various ELA Leadership Networks and collaborates with educators nationwide to address the challenges of the Common Core Standards. The Tips and Tricks Series is among several Common Core resources she has authored for Rosen Publishing.

Robin W. Parente is a practicing reading specialist and classroom teacher with over fifteen years of experience teaching reading and writing at the elementary level. She also serves as the elementary ELA coordinator for a medium-sized district in central New York, working with classroom teachers to implement best literacy practices in the classroom. Parente earned a BS in elementary education and an MS in education/literacy from the State University of New York at Oswego. She is a certified reading specialist (pre-K–12) and elementary classroom teacher and has served on various ELA Leadership Networks to collaborate with educators to address the challenges of the Common Core Standards. The Tips and Tricks Series is among several Common Core resources she has authored for Rosen Publishing.

Photo Credits

Cover © iStockphoto.com/RapidEye; pp. 4–5 Dean Mitchell/E+/Getty Images; p. 8 Blend Images/Hill Street Studios/Vetta/Getty Images; p. 13 Buyenlarge/Archive Photos/Getty Images; p. 19 PhotoQuest/Archive Photos/Getty Images; p. 24 Kurt Hutton/Picture Post/Getty Images; p. 28 Courtesy Everett Collection; p. 35 Stock Montage/Archive Photos/Getty Images; p. 41 © AP Images; p. 44 Henry Guttmann/Hulton Archive/Getty Images; p. 48 Hulton Archive/Getty Images; p. 51 PhotoTalk/E+/Getty Images; icons © iStockphoto.com/sodafish, © iStockphoto.com/mystockicons, © iStockphoto.com/Tantoon Studio, iStockphoto.com/sjhaytov, © iStockphoto.com/Aaltazar, © iStockphoto.com/Alex Belomlinsky.

Designer: Nicole Russo; Editor: Bethany Bryan;
Photo Researcher: Karen Huang